GOLIATH WITHIN

Winning the Battle of the Heart

Blessings!

Darlene Thorne

by Matthew 6:33

Darlene L. Thorne

Darlene Thorne

Edited by CreateSpace
Book and Cover design by Pixel
ISBN: 978-0-9960498-3-2

First Edition: August 2016

C O N T E N T S

Introduction   1

In Acknowledgment

Why We Battle   13

Who is the Real Enemy?   32

The Fear Factor   39

This Issue of Rejection   51

I Haven't Got Time for the Pain   67

The Weapon of Faith   77

The Weapon of Love   88

The Weapon of Prayer   99

The Weapon of Praise and Worship   109

Affirmations to Victory

About the Author

In Acknowledgement

For the many people in my life who have influenced me, pushed me, motivated me and inspired me to bring this book to fruition.
To all my coaches that have poured into my life I would like to thank you all for speaking into my life and encouraging me not to give up. I will never forget follow the lessons you all have taught me. Each one of you have taught me in a variety of ways about focus, locating the main thing in ministry, discipline and structure. Some of you have helped me put systems in place that allows me to be more deliberate and intentional in fulfilling God's call on my life.

To my mentors, I thank you all for showing me how to prioritize, set things in order and do the right thing at the right time. God's timing is so perfect and He knew when it was time for our paths to cross. You all have poured into me in so many ways and I will be forever grateful. I started to name people who have walked with me while I was in the writing process and the list got longer and longer! I knew at that point that I was going to leave someone out so I want to say a huge "Thank You" to all of my friends and family that helped to keep me on task, especially my accountability partners, I so appreciate your push!

To my Grace Worship Center Church family, you all are fantastic and I am blessed to be on this ministry journey with you. To my family members, I know I have the absolute greatest family in the world! Our hearts are knitted together. I love each and every one of you.

To my loving husband Kevin, a godly man who constantly tells me that I can do it, I love you with all my heart. You checked on me and my progress, even giving me some insight as I was walking through the writing process.

Your words of wisdom helped me focus on the important things. This has not been the easiest book to write for it caused me to really do a lot of self evaluation. With you there walking with me, the journey is one filled with triumphs!

My world changer children - Kevin, II and Kennedy Elayne, you two are radiant lights and I am thankful that God gave you both to us.

Introduction

Growing up as a preacher's daughter had its great moments, I was able to sit up front at concerts with famous singers because my dad invited them. I got to get home before everyone else did because we lived at the parsonage of the church which right behind the pulpit of the church. I would even sometimes hear what my father was going to preach about if I happened to be in the room when he and my mother were discussing the message. However, I think the biggest perk I got, in hindsight, was the fact that unless I was extremely ill, I never missed a Sunday service, Midweek Bible study, girls bible study with Sister Irma or my mother if she could not come. For that matter, I never missed anything that had to do with Emmanuel Tabernacle Assembly of God!

My mother never let us go without having family prayer every Sunday morning.

Whether it was all four of us children or not, we had prayer and the word… She taught us how important knowing God's word is for our lives. I may not have been as obedient as I should have, but one thing was for sure, the word of God had been deep seeded in my heart. I could not get away.

Yet with all the word that had been placed in me, I sometimes struggled with living in victory.

As I grew older and more grounded in my relationship with God, it was easy for me to give a word of encouragement to my sister or brother. I remember quoting scripture so easily and fluid like. " I can do all things through Christ which strengtheneth me," (Philippians 4:13 KJV) I could tell my friends that God was greater than any problem we faced. I had all the answers for everyone else except for me. How could I tell everyone else what God can do and how he would hear and answer their prayers but I could not seem to get over those hurdles myself? What was wrong with me? Did

I do something wrong in my Christian life? What was going on? I realized that I could help other people and encourage them but I struggled on the inside because even though I knew the word, applying the words to my life was a totally different thing.

When faced with obstacles in our Christian lives we have to be certain of our ability to overcome those situations we face. God has given us all of the tools to be over comers. However, He wants us to use these tools properly, consistently, and intentionally. We are going to explore some of the obstacles we face that may be preventing us from walking in full victory. We will examine issues such as fear, doubt, inadequacy, rejection and pain; how they manifest in our lives and what we can do to overcome them.

It will be work, it may not be easy. However, if we do the work shall reap the reward. It is not impossible yet it does take due diligence. Our heart and our mind must come into agreement with God's word in order to receive what He has promised.

I am grateful for an opportunity to share with you from the word of God how to be victorious despite the circumstances of life. You see, we have been created to live in victory, and we must do what is necessary to bring it to fruition. Even in writing this book, I encountered many obstacles that tried to prevent it from being written, but I had to persevere and push because I knew that many others need to be empowered.

I am grateful that God has seen fit to allow me to write these words of encouragement. My prayer is that you'll receive what is necessary to overcome the obstacles, circumstances and inward battles that will cause you to be better for the kingdom of God and impact those around you.

CHAPTER ONE

Why We Battle

In the Bible, David and Goliath are two people in who were at odds with each other. They were out to defeat each other. Interestingly enough, they did not know each other. They had no idea who the other was. All David knew was that he was on his way to make a delivery to his brothers and he walks into something he had not anticipated. Goliath was a tall dude who was a bully with a lot of talk. This is what gets me though: for a guy to be as tall as he was and had the heaviest of army gear, why had he not wiped out the army a long time ago? He had the ability, or at least one would think, to walk into the enemy camp and squash the men in their tents! In I Samuel chapter 17 we get a description of what Goliath looked like coming into battle.

"Then Goliath, a Philistine champion from Gath, came out of the Philistine

13

ranks to face the forces of Israel. He was over nine feet[a] tall! He wore a bronze helmet, and his bronze coat of mail weighed 125 pounds. He also wore bronze leg armor, and he carried a bronze javelin on his shoulder. The shaft of his spear was as heavy and thick as a weaver's beam, tipped with an iron spearhead that weighed 15 pounds. His armor bearer walked ahead of him carrying a shield." (I Samuel 17:4-7)[1]

And this is how he went to face the Israelites on a daily basis! He would come out and taunt them, him and probably his side kick/armor bearer, I will call him Bruno, to be there yelling all kinds of insults at them. He had someone hanging out there with him while he was talking to those who were in fact smaller than he was and they did not have that kind of armor.

---

[1] Holy Bible, New Living Translation copyright 1996, 2004, 2015 by Tyndale House Foundation. Used by permission of Tyndale House Publishers Inc., Carol Stream, Illinois 60188. All rights reserved.

He could have easily thrown the javelin or any of his pieces at the camp and it could have been over! What a bully! He talked junk every day for 40 days and the Israelites were shaking in their boots and never moved from their tents. They did not do anything but brood amongst themselves. You know, they could have gotten together and as an army attacked Goliath despite what he had said. But they were afraid. All of them were afraid, that is, except for David, and he was not even a part of the army!

David, a man after God's own heart, had been anointed as king at the age of 17 but did not take the throne until he was almost 30 years old was the youngest of Jesse's boys. He had only been going to the place of the battle to deliver food and check on his older brothers Eliab, Abinadab and Shammah. He had no knowledge of what was going on in Judah. His assignment was to deliver food and take the report back to his father. David had been anointed as king, but here he was delivering food and taking care of sheep - still. Let's take a look at how David got to be anointed as king in the first place.

When Samuel the prophet came to David's house, his father Jesse was told to get all of his children together because God was going to anoint a king from his household. (You can read of this account in I Samuel 16). All of the sons except David came and none of them were chosen. Samuel could have thought at first he heard the wrong instruction from God because not one of those guys were chosen. He asked Jesse if that was it, were there any others? I think Jesse had so many sons he may have thought they were all there or he may have presumed he knew what kind of man Samuel was looking for and he discounted David because he was young and didn't fit the bill. **SIDE NOTE**: Have you ever felt like that, that you didn't fit the bill?

"And Samuel said unto Jesse, Are here all thy children? And he said, There remaineth yet the youngest, and, behold, he keepeth the sheep. And Samuel said unto Jesse, Send and fetch him: for we will not sit down till he come hither. And he sent, and brought him in. Now he was ruddy, and withal of a beautiful countenance, and goodly to look to. And the Lord said, Arise, anoint him: for this is he." I Samuel 16: 11-12 KJV

David was a shepherd, he tended the flock and that kept him out in the fields most days. He was responsible for the safety of his father's livestock. This was not an easy undertaking. There were wolves and other animals that would try to kill the sheep so David's job was tough. I would imagine though he did have some time out there in the field to do some reflection and even some writing. He played a harp and it must have been some really good strumming because David was sent to see the king on several occasions. King Saul became vexed in his spirit. The king's servants spoke about David and his ability to play.

"And Saul's servants said unto him, Behold now, an evil spirit from God troubleth thee.

Let our Lord now command thy servants, which are before thee, to seek out a man, who is a cunning player on an harp: and it shall come to pass, when the evil spirit from God is upon thee, that he shall play with his hand, and thou shalt be well.

And Saul said unto his servants, Provide me now a man that can play well, and bring him to me.

Then answered one of the servants, and said, Behold, I have seen a son of Jesse the Bethlehemite, that is cunning in playing, and a mighty valiant man,

and a man of war, and prudent in matters, and a comely person, and the Lord
is with him." I Samuel 16: 15-18 KJV

Even though David was not the most
muscular or looked like he fit the mold for a
king, I mean what king plays a harp? Isn't that
for the Malcolm Milktoast type of guy? Yet
David was *the* chosen one to be the king.
However, even though he was the chosen one,
it was still a number of years before he took the
throne. He was the set man to go to minister
to Saul in his time of depression. You see depression isn't something new. Saul, yes King
Saul suffered from depression.

He became overwhelmed with the lead-
ership of the people. Have you ever felt un-
easy about doing something especially when
you thought there was someone more qualified
than yourself to carry it out? You may have
gotten butterflies in your stomach or you may
have had sweaty hands; whatever it was, you

thought that someone else was supposed to be in your place.

Martijn Huisman takes a look at the plight of King Saul and here is his observation:

> "This context is Saul's war against the Philistines. From the start it is quite clear that Saul faces extremely unfavorable odds. His people panic when the Philistine army gathers before them, which is not surprising, as Saul's core army amounts to about 3000 men, while the Philistine army consists of "thirty thousand chariots, and six thousand horsemen, and people as the sand which is on the seashore in multitude" (1 Samuel 13.5). Furthermore, Saul has been ordered by the religious leader Samuel to wait for his arrival after the hostilities have started, so that Samuel will make it known what Saul must do. Samuel, as Israel's religious

leader, speaks for God. Ignoring his order is out of the question.

Clearly, the demands are extremely high: fighting a war against all odds, keeping his frightened soldiers under control and facing what appears to be almost certain defeat. Saul's control over the situation is obviously minimal. Before he can actually take action, Saul needs to wait for the arrival of Samuel (for 7 days!)so that he can be told what course of action to follow.

In the end, Saul cannot bear the stress and he does what is forbidden to him. He starts by giving burnt offerings to God, in order to gain his favor in battle. However, giving burnt offerings was traditionally a domain preserved for the priests and hence was forbidden to the king. When Samuel finally arrives, he reprimands Saul severely. Samuel says: "thou hast done foolishly: thou hast not kept the commandment of the Lord thy God, which he commanded thee: [...] now thy kingdom shall not continue [...]" (1 Samuel 13.13–14).Subsequently, Saul begins to display the well–known signs of depression."[2]

King Saul's depression was soothed by David's playing of the harp. David ministered to the soul of a man suffering. He was able to calm the demons in King Saul because he was anointed to do just that. David was not only an anointed harpist, he as also a fighter. As the one who was responsible for the sheep, he had to protect them from dangerous animals. The Bible speaks of instances that David killed a lion and a bear. In I Samuel 17: 34-36, David explains to Saul his ability to take on Goliath,

But David said to Saul, "Your servant was tending his father's sheep. When a

---

[2] J Epidemiol Community Health. 2007 Oct; 61(10): 890

lion or a bear came and took a lamb from the flock, I went out after him and attacked him, and rescued it from his mouth; and when he rose up against me, I seized him by his beard and struck him and killed him. Your servant has killed both the lion and the bear; and this uncircumcised Philistine will be like one of them, since he has taunted the armies of the living God."

David likened Goliath to the lion and the bear. He had no problem going after him and defeating him because he was going to have the back of those who belonged to God. He was not afraid to defeat this foe, he was not walking in his own strength, he was walking in the power of God!

This is so interesting especially when we know that David would be hiding from his own army and wondering about who he was and if God was with him (but that is a little later in this reading).

The Masoretic Text, the Hebrew text that has long been accepted by the Jewish people, states that Goliath's height was "six cubits and one span." Taking a cubit to be approximately eighteen inches and a span to equal six, this figures to a height of approximately nine feet, six inches. Other studies have purported that Goliath stood about six feet five inches which was still taller than most of the population at that time.

Why are David and Goliath fighting? Because the Philistines have proposed to send their toughest warrior against the Israelites' toughest warrior to settle a dispute in "single combat." As Gladwell put it in his TED talk:

> The Philistine who is sent down, their mighty warrior, is a giant. ... He's outfitted head to toe in this glittering bronze armor, and he's got a sword and he's got a javelin and he's got his spear. He is absolutely terrifying. And he's so terrifying that none of the Israelite soldiers

want to fight him. It's a death wish, right? There's no way they think they can take him.

On the other hand, David is a lowly shepherd boy--and yet he's the only person willing to fight Goliath. He also refuses to wear armor. Why? Because David is also apparently the only person in the story who realizes that heavy armor weighs a warrior down. Goliath could easily kill David with his sword-- but only if David were foolish enough to walk right up to Goliath. Of course, that's the last thing David plans to do.[3]

David and Goliath had no real beef with each other, they were protecting their land and their people. It was not about them because they did not know each other. They had to save their people. The battle was never about them, but the focus shifted to them because the lesson

---

[3] 3 Things People Get Wrong About David vs. Goliath by Bill Murphy Jr., TheMid.com published May 6, 2014

learned here is to show how the Lord inter-cedes for His people. Goliath was taunting God's people and David had faith in God to be-lieve God would deliver the people. God is able, yes, well able to deliver.

> "From the story of David and Goliath, we can learn that the God we serve is capable of defeating any of the giants in our lives—fear, depression, financial issues, doubts of faith—if we know Him and His nature well enough to step out in faith. When we do not know what the future holds, we have to trust Him. But we can't trust someone we don't know, so knowing God through His Word will build our faith in Him.[4]

Similar to David, our battle is not with those around us, our battle is that inner struggle to be free and to fulfill our God given assignment. Even David, after defeating Goliath had to live

---

[4]"What Should we Learn From the Account of David and Goliath?" Got Questions Ministries, n.d. Web. 01 June 2016

with the inner struggles and found his greatest victory through one of my favorite weapons, praise and worship! He was able to bring victory to the people of Israel, yet he found himself having to fight his own demons, sounds familiar, huh? We can help everyone else get victory and we go home hoping someone would call us and no one does. We battle because we are sometimes afraid to: ask for help, don't know WHO to ask for help, pride (because we think someone will think less of us if we ask for help), fear (people will see that we don't have it all together).

NOTES

_____

_____

_____

_____

_____

_____

_____

_____

_____

_____

_____

_____

_____

_____

_____

_____

_____

_____

_____

_____

_____

_____

NOTES

NOTES

NOTES

_____

_____

_____

_____

_____

_____

_____

_____

_____

_____

_____

_____

_____

_____

_____

_____

_____

_____

_____

_____

_____

CHAPTER TWO
<u>The Real Enemy</u>

When we were children and we got in trouble with our parents we sometimes were with our siblings when something either broke or was damaged and no one wanted to admit who the culprit was that committed the misdeed. We may have been the guilty one but we tell our siblings not to snitch. If that happened in our house, everyone was punished! When the parents cannot get a straight answer, everyone paid the price.

If we are in covenant with God we must realize that not all the time is it our brother or sister in or out of Christ that is the doer of an injustice to ourselves. The devil, Satan, Lucifer, the demon himself may very well be at the bottom of it all and we go blaming others for it. The devil is good at using people to mess with the people of God. He does his best to separate us one from another.

The Bible states that he comes to kill, steal and destroy! That is his job! He wants to kill our dreams, our plans, our family members with either physical or spiritual death. He wants to steal our joy, our peace, our witness, he wants to rob us of our finances, our health, etc,. His desire is to truly sift us as wheat. If the devil has his way he will attempt to destroy us and our witness, he wants to make us feel like we should not say anything because of the mistakes we may have made. We are ashamed without realizing that in spite of our mistakes we are to move because that is what truly brings glory to God.

The focus is not on us and what we could do, but on God and what He did do! I heard this line that God can make a message out of a mess! When we turn over every thing to God, we give Him control to work in us what we need and work out of us what is not necessary for our lives to be used for His Kingdom! We are here for God's glory and so the things we suffer are not for us but they are for God to be magnified and us to decrease.

Remember that we are here for God's glory and to display His character. If we will not give in to the devil and his imps, we will see victory over our circumstances. We have to maintain our trust in God and submit to His direction. In this way, we win. When we submit to God, the devil will flee. However, we at times think we have the better solution. We try, we fail and then we come to God, like a child with a broken toy, we ask God to fix it. God is always there to repair the damage. We must realize, though, sometimes in repairing the damage it can appear to be painful.

NOTES

_____

_____

_____

_____

_____

_____

_____

_____

_____

_____

_____

_____

_____

_____

_____

_____

_____

_____

NOTES

NOTES

_____

_____

_____

_____

_____

_____

_____

_____

_____

_____

_____

_____

_____

_____

_____

_____

_____

_____

_____

NOTES

_____

_____

_____

_____

_____

_____

_____

_____

_____

_____

_____

_____

_____

_____

_____

_____

_____

_____

_____

CHAPTER THREE

The Fear Factor

Perfect love casts out fear...'The one who fears is not made perfect in love. Such love has no fear, because perfect love expels all fear. If we are afraid, it is for fear of punishment, and this shows that we have not fully experienced his perfect love. There is no fear in love, but perfect love casts out fear.'[5]

If we truly love God then we will operate as He does. When Jesus walked this earth, He feared no man and He did only as the Father instructed Him. When God told Jesus that He was not to take the crown and be made king when the people wanted Him to be king Jesus disappeared into the crowd. However, by the same token, when Jesus came into the synagogue and the money changers were swindling the people so they would buy their

---

[5] biblehub.com/1_john/4-18.htm

sacrifices from them, Jesus went rogue! He beat them out of the place telling them they have made the house of the Lord a den of thieves! How could the people think they would get away with that!

Jesus was not afraid, He was confident in His calling and what He knew was right. The people were taking advantage of the citizens and Jesus was not having it. He was defending those who could not speak for themselves. They may have felt powerless to stand up against those who told them their sacrifices were not good enough. They may have already been a little nervous about coming to bring their sacrifices in the first place, then when they arrive at the synagogue they are told their sacrifice was not fit, I am pretty sure they were more than happy even though they had to pay money for the dove or whatever sacrifice they were bringing they probably thought it was better than it not being received.

Think about it. These people were afraid to bring their own sacrifice to the temple because they did not think it was good enough. Here we go again, making it all about us. Those money changers were only there to make themselves rich. They knew the animals the people were bringing were okay because they already knew what was required of them. They were to bring a spotless animal to the temple and according to some commentaries they mentioned that if it were in the interest of the priest to get the people to spend their money it would go to them and the priests that may have been in agreement with the money changers. They would be milking the people of their hard earned money and making them feel guilty about the sacrifices they brought with them.

What things do we fear and why do we fear them? For the most part we fear things that we have not encountered and we're ignorant as to what they can do or the power that one might seem to possess over us. We fear things that may or may not be real. We tend not to be as fearful of a lion in a cage; as a matter of fact, we may even tease the lion and talk about how odd he might look. We don't stand frozen, why, because there is glass or in some cases there are bars that separate us from the lion.

But if someone were to have accidentally flipped a switch and the bars and glass were removed, tell me how many of us would remain in that space even if the lion did not ever move from where he was? See, all we may have seen was the bars and glass go up; but what we did not take the time to examine was the back left ankle of the lion was chained and he could not move, even if he wanted to. But since we did not see it, we immediately took off.

Sometimes in our Christian walk those fears are just like that, we are afraid of something that has no power over us. The Bible clearly states in I John 4:18, "There is no fear in love. But perfect love **drives out fear,** because fear has to do with punishment. The one who fears is not made perfect in love." Perfect love or a mature love does not have fear attached to it. Fear is dissipated. If we truly love God and are committed to fulfilling His will for our lives then there is not any room for fear. There is no room for any hesitation in moving toward the place God has set for us.

Psalm 3:6 says, "I will not fear though tens of thousands assail me on every side."

People Fear

We fear people because of what we think they will say about us behind our backs. We are fearful of whether or not we will make a fool or ourselves when we get on the stage. We sometimes will not make a phone call to ask for something because we think they will say no. This is the funny thing though, people may talk about you whether or not you do something.   We also do not know what response we may get from a person, we have made a decision for them which is really not our call.

Sometimes we have conversations in our heads saying how we think the other person might respond based upon how we are feeling. If we are fearful, we will probably have a conversation that will end negatively. We decide to call anyway after we have determined in our head how the conversation will go and nine times out of ten we are correct. We hang up the phone saying something like, "I knew it!" But in all actuality, if you replayed the call and thought about what you said, your own words may have been the reason you received the response that came from the person you called.

We cannot afford to be fearful. We have a responsibility and a job to do and fear cannot be anywhere around us.   Joyce Meyer said that we should do it afraid, so even it fear tries to raise its ugly head, we must move in spite of it. Jesus told his disciples in Matthew 28:20b, "And surely I am with you always, to the very end of the age." He also told them in John 14: 26-27,

> "But the Advocate, the Holy Spirit, whom the Father will send in my name, will teach you all things and will remind you of everything I have said to you. Peace I leave with you; my peace I give you. I do not give to you as the world gives. Do not let your hearts be troubled and do not be afraid."

You must be clear in your spirit that no matter what, you choose to be obedient to God and what He says and not man. On Judgment Day we all stand alone before His face. He will not give us a pass because we tell Him that we were afraid of what someone else might have said about us.

I Thessalonians 2: 4 says, 'On the contrary, we speak as those approved by God to be entrusted with the gospel. We are not trying to please people but God, who tests our hearts.' Our allegiance is to the one we serve. We are not here to serve man, we are here to have dominion and bring the good news of the gospel to a dying world. We are charged to use our gifts, whatever they are to be used to draw someone to make a decision to allow God to be Lord of their lives. So what we do on earth should not be seen as competing with one another if the end goal is the same. We are called to be a part of kingdom building. We can count it a privilege to be chosen and do what we do with humility, excellence and in the authority of the one who gave us the assignment in the beginning.

NOTES

NOTES

_____

_____

_____

_____

_____

_____

_____

_____

_____

_____

_____

_____

_____

_____

_____

_____

_____

_____

NOTES

_____
_____
_____
_____
_____
_____
_____
_____
_____
_____
_____
_____
_____
_____
_____
_____
_____
_____
_____
_____
_____

NOTES

CHAPTER FOUR

<u>*The Issue of Rejection*</u>

What do we spend most of our time focusing on? Matthew 19:21-22 says, Jesus answered, "If you want to be perfect, go, sell your possessions and give to the poor, and you will have treasure in heaven. Then come, follow me." When the young man heard this, he went away sad, because he had great wealth. His focus was on what he had and not what he could gain.

Are we focusing on the seed we have now and are afraid to plant it? We are not thinking long term then...we plant now for a greater harvest!

We have the ability to make a decision that will affect our future. Maybe we think we are like the dog who was looking in the water seeing his reflection and tried to grab the bone from "the other dog". Maybe we are afraid to launch out because we think we may sabotage our success or we might also be thinking, what if it works? Success can be just as frightening.

Either way, however, we will never know the results if we do nothing. One thing is for certain, if you do nothing you will get nothing! If you do not move you are going backwards and will be left behind. Time stands still for no one and if you do not move you have wasted both time and talent. We have been given abilities to do many things, whether it is writing, speaking, being a great administrator or an organizer, having a love for caring for the elderly or children. You can even have a passion for dogs, it does not matter what that thing is, it matters what you do with that thing you are most passionate about.

You cannot afford to keep those things to yourself. Someone needs what you have. Even if you are one of those people that gives someone else a good kick in the pants to move to be in better health, you are necessary!! Stop waiting in the wings for someone to call your name! Call your own name and walk out on stage to fulfill your God-given destiny. You are not too late! It is time for you to move. Maybe you are asking how do I get started?

1. First, write down what it is you are passionate about. Writing it out helps to put feet to the vision. When you see a logo of the Nike swish, you immediately think of what? yes, you are right, "Just Do It". The marketing gurus know that you must have something that will make people remember their company. When you write down what you are passionate about and you put it in a place where you will always see it, man it does something to your insides. You see it every day and yo get inspired. But it is not enough to just write it down.

2. Secondly, find someone trustworthy with which to share your passion. It can be a family member or a friend, that is not the most important thing about this exercise. The most important thing about this is the fact that you should share this with that person that you trust and can know they will encourage you to go for it. They will become your source of encouragement and help keep you motivated when you think you cannot go on.

3. Prayer is so important in this new journey. Your ability to move forward has to have a foundation of prayer and the scriptures from God's word to keep you going in the right direction. The scriptures say that without a vision the people perish and that we are to take every thing to God and seek Him for wisdom in how to carry out the task set before us.

The Reticular Activating System (RAS)

The reticular activating system (RAS) is the portal through which nearly all information enters the brain.

Your reticular activating system is like a filter between your conscious mind and your subconscious mind. It takes instructions from your conscious mind and passes them on to your subconscious. For example, the instruction might be, "listen out for anyone saying my name".

There are some interesting points about your RAS that make it an essential tool for achieving goals.

First, you can deliberately program the reticular activating system by choosing the exact messages you send from your conscience mind. For example, you can set goals, or say affirmations, or visualize your goals. Napoleon Hill said that we can achieve any realistic goal if we keep on thinking of that goal, and stop thinking any negative thoughts about it. Of course, if we keep thinking that we can't achieve a goal, our subconscious will help us NOT achieve it.

Second, your reticular activating system cannot distinguish between 'real events' and 'synthetic' reality. In other words it tends to believe whatever message you give it. Imagine that you're going to be giving a speech. You can practice giving that speech by visualizing it in your mind. This 'pretend' practice should improve your ability to give the speech.

In his classic 1960 self-help book, *Psychocybernetics*, Dr. Maxwell Maltz discusses our automatic goal seeking 'servo-mechanism'. He doesn't use the words reticular activating system, but it is the same process. What we need to do is to create a very specific picture of our goal in our conscious mind. The RAS will then pass this on to our subconscious - which will then help us achieve the goal. It does this by bringing to our attention all the relevant information which otherwise might have remained as 'background noise'.[6]

Our bodies are very intelligent machines and the brain is very sensitive equipment. What we tell ourselves on a consistent basis is usually what we will act out. It is so important that we speak life to our circumstances. We

---

[6] Copyright: Make-Your-Goals-Happen.com

cannot afford to speak death and defeat to our dreams and desires. When loving parents talk with their children about how they will fair in school, how many of them tell their children that they are going to be failures and that they will not succeed? How often do you hear them say that they are not going to learn anything and they do not care if they go to school or not because it won't make a difference? That does not happen too often, right? Yes, parents speak life to their children; they tell them to work hard and if the child says something like they can't, the parent almost immediately disregards that negative talk and encourages their child that they can do it and that there is not anything they cannot accomplish. They speak life to the child. It is almost instinctive to do this because the parent knows if they let their child wallow in their feelings the child will get what they have been thinking about.

The Bible speaks of what comes from our mouth in many different passages. The scriptures on the next pages are just a few verses that would be beneficial to memorize for your spiritual growth and to empower you to believe in yourself. You are special and impor- tant to the Kingdom!

On the next pages as you reflect on these writ- ings, what things will you give to God that you had been holding onto? What will you choose to focus on to change the environment in which you live? Write your thoughts and your prayer as a marker of the new path you are choosing to denounce rejection.

NOTES

NOTES

_____

_____

_____

_____

_____

_____

_____

_____

_____

_____

_____

_____

_____

_____

_____

_____

_____

_____

_____

_____

_____

NOTES

NOTES

_____

_____

_____

_____

_____

_____

_____

_____

_____

_____

_____

_____

_____

_____

_____

_____

_____

_____

_____

_____

For Your Time of Meditation

James 3:5b-8 "How great a forest is set ablaze by such a small fire! And the tongue is a fire, a world of unrighteousness. The tongue is set among our members, staining the whole body, setting on fire the entire course of life, and set on fire by hell. For every kind of beast and bird, of reptile and sea creature, can be tamed and has been tamed by mankind, but no human being can tame the tongue. It is a restless evil, full of deadly poison. With it we bless our Lord and Father, and with it we curse people who are made in the likeness of God."

Proverbs 18:21 "Death and life are in the power of the tongue, and those who love it will eat its fruits."

Matthew 12:36-27 "I tell you, on the day of judgment people will give account for every careless word they speak, for by your words you will be justified, and by your words you will be condemned."

Matthew 12:33-35 "Either make the tree good and its fruit good, or make the tree bad and its fruit bad, for the tree is known by its fruit. You brood of vipers! How can you speak good, when you are evil? For out of the abundance of the heart the mouth speaks. The good person out of his good treasure brings forth good, and the evil person out of his evil treasure brings forth evil."

Ephesians 4:29 "Let no corrupting talk come out of your mouths, but only such as is good for building up, as fits the occasion, that it may give grace to those who hear."

Proverbs 12:18 "There is one whose rash words are like sword thrusts, but the tongue of the wise brings healing."

Proverbs 13:3 "Whoever guards his mouth preserves his life; he who opens wide his lips comes to ruin."

Proverbs 15:4 "A wholesome tongue [is] a tree of life: but perverseness therein [is] a breach in the spirit."

Proverbs 16:23 "From a wise mind comes wise speech; the words of the wise are per-suasive."

Luke 6:45 "The good person out of the good treasure of his heart produces good, and the evil person out of his evil treasure produces evil, for out of the abundance of the heart his mouth speaks."

NOTES

CHAPTER FIVE

I Haven't Got Time for the Pain

"Where does it hurt?", the doctor asks. "Everywhere!" is the response. Sometimes we just hurt and we cannot explain it. That feeling of total loss, defeat and misery. We feel like there is no way we are going to bounce back from this one. We say it is too hard, it hurts too much and we retreat.

I remember feeling that way when I thought I was doing the right things, I was moving along in ministry and I knew I had heard from the Lord regarding the direction He wanted me to go. I thought I was really hearing God speaking to me and I thought I was following the path God had for me. However, in the midst of this I was blindsided with something that was extremely hurtful and painful to me. This is a hard story to tell because I do not want to bring attention to any person or persons. When serving in ministry it is so important to be at the ready when called upon to serve.

In my case I thought I was doing just that and when I was told otherwise, it was as if someone had come and put a pin in my balloon. Now I will tell you this, if you saw me, you would never know that there was ever anything going on. Why? Because like some of you reading this book are great at hiding. I hid behind my smile, but my heart was in so much pain. What added insult to injury is that there was no one at the time that I could talk to about the situation.

Not that there was not a person to talk with, but because the pain was so deep, there was no place to begin! Such pain and confusion, I couldn't figure out why this was happening. I remember asking for clarity and each time I received different explanations. I recall crying out to God asking Him what was happening, I was asking Him to reveal to me the error of my ways to ask for cleansing-I heard nothing. I went before the Lord about this as it seemed many times asking Him for some revelation.

When I did hear from God regarding this situation I heard Him tell me that I was in this place to see how to continue to stay in His presence no matter what comes or goes. I had not done anything wrong, God was simply showing me that just as He had been wrongfully accused and His response was nothing, so should my response be. I was in good company. I learned from that situation to pray for anyone who may intentionally or unintentionally mistreat me even though it may have been painful. The Bible says that vengeance belonged to God and He would repay. It was not for me to try and figure it out. I am to forgive, love and treat them like God would want us to treat them.

You see sometimes we take on issues that are not ours. We actually are being kind of vain when we think it is about us. Sometimes we are the vessel God desires to use to sharpen someone else. When we don't pay evil for evil and we still smile at the person who has done something to cause us pain, we are living out the scripture that says it is like heaping coals of fire on their heads. It is not up to us to "make them pay" that is up to God. He knows ahead of time what we are going through and He will take care of the situations. We are to be God pleasers in all we do.

The Father desires our earnest commitment to Him and His plans for our lives. We are to 'work out our soul salvation with fear and trembling' (Philippians 2:12). Some of you may ask what that means; the Amplified Bible explains that portion of scripture like this - [that is, cultivate it, bring it to full effect, actively pursue spiritual maturity] with awe-inspired fear and trembling [using serious caution and critical self-evaluation to avoid anything that might offend God or discredit the name of Christ]. Our goal should always be to bring glory to God.

The focus is not on us but on what He wants to accomplish in the earth through us His servants. In the book, '*The Purpose Driven Life*' by Pastor Rick Warren, the first line of chapter one says this, "It's not about you." I will not forget when I read those words. They stung.

I was looking for my purpose and I thought it was about me finding out what I was supposed to do. Really it is about me seeking God for Him to reveal to me what to do. I do not create the plan and ask God to bless it; no, I go to Him and ask Him how I can best serve in the Kingdom through the gifts He placed in me. I bring myself into subjection and allow Him to work in me to do His bidding. We get it mixed up thinking God is just supposed to answer our prayers no matter what we ask, He will just be at our beck and call. Nothing can be farther from the truth.

God wants us to give back to Him what He gave to us in order for us to reach the lost. It is His kingdom come, it is His will be done in earth as it is in heaven. When I look at the words "in earth," I think about us His creation. We were created from the dust of the earth, so when He said that His will be done in earth, I see it as let His will be done in US as it is done in heaven. Allow His will to be worked out of us. Because He is the Divine Manufacturer He knows how we are to function. Wouldn't it be so simple to consult the Creator who knows better than us trying to figure it out?

On the next few pages write out those painful situations that you are turning over to God and your prayer of release. Forgive those who inflicted pain and bless them by using the word of God, bless those who mistreat you.

NOTES

NOTES

NOTES

_____

_____

_____

_____

_____

_____

_____

_____

_____

_____

_____

_____

_____

_____

_____

_____

_____

_____

_____

NOTES

CHAPTER SIX

___The Weapon of Faith___

While we have heard about faith being important to our Christian walk, I am wondering how seriously we take activating our faith as a weapon. So many times we may talk about faith, quoting scripture because many of us know it by heart, "Now faith is the substance of things hoped for, the evidence of things not seen.." (Hebrews 11:1 KJV) The word that sticks out for me is the word NOW. This word Now is very important in this scripture. You see, the verse could have easily read, "Faith is the substance...", why is it Now faith is? Faith is present active not passive. It is an ever moving and a constant as long as we will be the ones who will put 'faith' to work.

The New Living Translation states that faith is the "confidence" that what we hope for will actually happen; it gives us assurance about the things we cannot see. It is interesting we cannot see the wind, we cannot see cold or heat but we feel it. Our senses let us know when it is good to cover up and put on a coat or whether it is ok to go out without one. We believe these things are real although they are not visible. So why do we have so many issues with believing?

Faith is not seen but it is active. Faith is always at work whether it be positive or negative. Negative faith? Yes, I said negative faith! We can believe that we will be hurt or that nothing good will happen and we see those things come to pass. The Bible say that you will have what you say. Job said when he was experiencing his loss that the thing that he feared the most has come upon him. So, if Job could bring it to fruition how much more do we bring into manifestation those negative things because of what we speak and choose to believe?

How will someone know what you believe? The scriptures say that what is in the heart the mouth speaks. What do you say to yourself? To others? What do you find yourself speaking from day to day? Are you speaking life to yourself and others? When there is turmoil going on in your life how do you deal with it? Do you tend to focus on the problem or the one who can take care of the problem? God has told us that He is concerned about what is going on in our lives and as we lean on Him, He will never leave us nor forsake us. So if we know who is in control why do we not trust and have faith? I believe one of the reasons is because of our focus. The things we focus on get the most attention.

A good photographer is able to bring your attention to what they want you to see in a picture by the way they use the focus on with the lens. The picture could be a close-up of a person, but you can see clearly in the background a picture of a house. Why, because the photographer has adjusted the lens to target a particular object. He has practiced and spent time to get it right. The same should hold true for us-as we focus on the result and not the problem our ability to see the result becomes easier. When we speak good things that is what we begin to attract.

At the end of this chapter is a list of some positive confessions that I challenge you to make for the next 21 days. When you arise in the morning, have them in your bathroom and every room you pass through daily so you can see them while you are getting ready for the day.

There are also a couple of questions I would like for you to answer; there are no right or wrong answers, these are for you to ponder and pray about as you are renewing your mind. Philippians 4:8 says, "Brothers and sisters, continue to think about what is good and worthy of praise. Think about what is true and honorable and right and pure and beautiful and respected."[7]

On the next few pages I encourage you to look up verses in the Bible on faith and write them down. Then take one of those verses each week and memorize it. When the word of God is hidden in your heart, you strengthen your spirit being.

[7] ERV, Copyright © 2006 by Bible League International

FAITH CONFESSION

I AM A CONQUEROR

I AM VICTORIOUS

THERE IS NOTHING IMPOSSIBLE

WITH GOD

I CAN DO ALL THINGS THROUGH

GOD'S LOVE SURROUNDS ME

I AM AN OVERCOMER

I AM A HARD WORKER

I AM NOT A PROCASTINATOR

I KEEP THE MAIN THING THE MAIN

THING

I AM FOCUSED

I AM A TIMELY PERSON

GOD IS INTENTIONAL

NOTHING IS RANDOM

I BELIEVE GOD, I BELIEVE GOD, I

BELIEVE GOD

Questions to ponder:

1. What do I spend most of my time thinking about?

_____

_____

_____

_____

_____

_____

2. Are those thoughts positive or negative?

_____

_____

_____

_____

3. What will I do to renew my mind?

_____

_____

_____

_____

NOTES

NOTES

_____

_____

_____

_____

_____

_____

_____

_____

_____

_____

_____

_____

_____

_____

_____

_____

_____

_____

_____

_____

_____

NOTES

NOTES

CHAPTER SEVEN

The Weapon of Love

The Bible says that even if you have the ability to speak eloquently and do not have love you are nothing (Darlene's paraphrase). If we do not have love we are like sounding brass or a tinkling cymbal. We are like those who make a lot of noise and say nothing. Without the true love that God tells us to express to others we will never be able to truly fulfill the call we have on our lives. We will never fully express to the world and to those we have been called to what they need to hear to achieve their goals.

When we hold back from loving the way Christ loves us, someone always loses. Our Father desires that we be like those who will lay down our lives for one another, that we will prefer one another. Would it be so bad to let someone else get the spotlight? Are we so insecure that we are unwilling to give some shine on someone else?

The weapon of love is very critical to our success in defeating the Goliath's in our life. I Corinthians 13:5-7 talks about love like this:

"Love is patient and kind. Love is not jealous, it does not brag, and it is not proud. Love is not rude, it is not selfish, and it cannot be made angry easily. Love does not remember wrongs done against it. Love is never happy when others do wrong, but it is always happy with the truth. Love never gives up on people. It never stops trusting, never loses hope, and never quits."

What would your world look like if you chose to be patient, kind, and got rid of jealousy? How would you see yourself if you were not selfish and always talking about your accomplishments? When someone shares a victory, instead of trying to one-up them, celebrate them and save yours for another time? Oh here is a good one, how does it sound to you to truly forgive AND forget? Don't bring up someone's past mistake all the time. God is telling us through His word that we ought to pattern our lives after Him. When Jesus walked this earth, he was talked about, falsely accused, beaten up, hung on a cross for our sin, and in all of this, he was not guilty of any crime! Love is definitely a weapon that will destroy the devil.

When we love, we nullify fear, this aids in getting rid of doubt and unbelief.   Our love is to be genuine towards others. We can express our love towards others in several ways.

1. **Call someone and encourage them.** It does not have to be to congratulate them for something, it can be for the simple fact that you thought about them and you wanted to send them a word to motivate them to keep pushing. I remember doing this many times and just about every time I did, the response from toe person I encountered was that it was just what they needed! They appreciat-

ed the time I took to call them. Calling someone and talking, not texting, has become a lost art. When you take the time to pick up the phone and dial their number, it can really make a difference in a persons' life. I know I have gotten calls and they just said they wanted to see how I was doing and then they would give me a word of encouragement; it really blessed my soul!

2. **Send a card to someone in the mail.** Yes, take the time to handwrite a message and send it! What this actually does is cause us to have to take the time to pick out the appropriate card, and think about what you want to say. When we do this and send it off, I know for myself, it brought me a feeling of joy and peace. What was the icing on the cake was the response I received from the recipient! Some told me they cried, others said the message was right on time. Being sensitive to the Spirit of God makes all the difference in the world.

3. **Celebrate someone else's success open- ly.** These suggestions may sound a little cheesy but I guarantee you will be blessed by focusing on others. When you celebrate someone else you are actually living out the scriptures that tell us to prefer one another. Let me also say that our heart attitude will change as we lift up others. When we stop looking at our own situations with despair and celebrate others, what we are doing is planting seeds. If God can do it for them, I know He can do it for me. We rejoice with those that rejoice! Yes, we spend time cele- brating with others and God sees all, we make preparation for Him to bless us. That is not the reason we do it, however, it is a benefit we will reap because of it.

4. **Be honest, tell the truth, in love.** Some- times there are hard things that need to be said. In today's society so many people are wanting to be politically correct and letting others go down in flames! We say things

like, 'I saw it coming,' or 'I knew she or he should not have trusted them,' but we never said anything! We say that we don't want to hurt them or we don't want to kill their vibe, but they get hurt just the same because we said nothing. If we see our brother or sister about to go down a wrong path, in love, tell them! That is a true sign of love. Someone who loves will at least give fair warning. If they choose not to listen, at least fair waring was given. No one likes to hear that some-one else knew the plan would blow up in their face and they never told them. It can be taken that the person wanted them to fail so they withheld information. We must show love by sometimes saying what may not want to be heard, but true love will want to keep someone from danger or being hurt or from losing a monetary investment. The truth may sting, but if it will help prevent a person from falling, throw them a lifeline. In all of these suggestions notice that the focus is not us but others. They will know that we are Christians by the love we have one for another. We prefer one another and we lift up others for in due season we will be acknowledged and it will blow our minds because God does things BIG!

Who will you call and encourage over the next few weeks? Who will you send a card or note to over the next month? Who will you deliberately choose to celebrate for their accomplishments? Telling the truth in love can be a challenge, however, who will you share truth with in love over the next few days? On the pages that follow, prayerfully make out your list and follow through with reaching out to these individuals.

NOTES

NOTES

_____

_____

_____

_____

_____

_____

_____

_____

_____

_____

_____

_____

_____

_____

_____

_____

_____

_____

NOTES

NOTES

CHAPTER EIGHT

The Weapon of Prayer

One of the most powerful weapons we have in winning the inner battle is prayer! Prayer destroys the enemy and his tactics. Prayer releases the power of God. Prayers put in action the word of God. Praying brings us in agreement with God's word. When we pray we are speaking to the God of the universe, who created all things.

Why is prayer so important to our arsenal? Prayer is our communication with God. It is our dialogue with the one who created us and through Him all things exist. If we do not develop a habit of prayer and meditation, we cannot expect to defeat Satan. Satan is the robber and we cannot let him take what does not belong to him. He comes in many forms, however, one of the ways he comes is by planting negative and defeatist thoughts in our

minds. Just as in the beginning when Gd created Eve, the serpent came to her and chal-
lenged her by asking her what God said about
what she and Adam could do in the Garden.
He caused her to doubt God's words so much
and believe his, that she and Adam ate of the
tree of the knowledge of good and evil. When
she did that, the serpent was pleased that he
deceived her.

The Bible tells us in the book of Romans
chapter 12 that we are to renew our minds daily so that we can prove what is the good and
acceptable will of God. We prove what it is by
knowing what God's word says and praying it
into manifestation. When we read verses like,
'If ye be willing and obedient, ye shall eat the
good of the land," (Isaiah 1:19 KJV) and we
pray them in a manner like this,

"Lord, your word says that if I am willing and obedient, I shall eat the good of
the land. I thank you for your promise
and I choose to come in line with your

word to be both willing and obedient. I
know that I shall eat the good of the
land. All of my need shall be met, I will
not lack in any good thing for you God
are

Jehovah Jireh, my Provider. I thank you
Lord, in Jesus name, amen."

Our most powerful weapon is the word of God
in prayer. Yes, God hears us when we pray
our own words, but what better way to know
that we are in line with the will of God than to
pray that His will be done. What is His will?
His word is His will. There are several books
that I would like to recommend you consider
adding to your library in the area of prayer.
Books by author E. M. Bounds on prayer are
phenomenal. They are powerful to help you
understand various aspects of prayer. Some
titles of his books are:

*Power Through Prayer, Prayer and Praying
Men, The Essentials of Prayer, The Necessity*

of Prayer, The Possibilities of Prayer, Purpose in Prayer and The Weapon of Prayer.
Another author that has books on prayer is Germaine Copeland with a series on '*Prayers that Avail Much.*'

Prayer will be the key to your victory! Nothing is impossible with God and all things are possible through Him. He wants us to spend time in His presence so come with something to write with because He will speak. Jesus is a prime example for us to follow. He spent time in prayer to receive His instructions. He heard from His Father, as a matter of fact He said that He only does what He is instructed to do. When He spent time before the Lord God gave Him the plan to carry out. We have the word of God to prove that out. There are 66 books for us to see what God has done and will do. Our responsibility is to find out what part we play in fulfilling our assignment. I like this acronym in my prayer time: **A**cknowledge, **C**onfess, **T**hanksgiving, **S**upplication. Spend some time in acknowledging God for who He is; our Savior, Redeemer, Deliverer, Jehovah Jireh (our provider) Jehovah Rapha (our Healer), the Alpha and Omega, etc. Then it is come clean time. Repent for things like disobedience, attitudes that were ungodly, and anything that the Lord may show you. After you have emptied your heart of those sins and things that may block you from hearing from the Lord, thank Him for hearing your confessions and thank Him for all He has done. Lastly, you bring Him your requests. Here is where I believe it is okay to have your eyes open while in prayer. You are now praying God's word back to Him. We don't pray the problem, we pray God's solution! His solution is in His word! If it is healing you desire, it is by His stripes we are healed and we pray His word. This is why meditation and scripture study is so important. You want to find out what God says about your situations and pray the answer, for He already knows what we need before we ask. Use your weapon of prayer and experience an encounter like never before.

On the pages that follow, write out your prayers using the word of God for those things you are walking toward. The word of God is powerful and mighty to change the environment. Use God's word to impact your world. Writing out the word of God helps you to memorize what He says about us.

NOTES

_____

_____

_____

_____

_____

_____

_____

_____

_____

_____

_____

_____

_____

_____

_____

_____

_____

_____

NOTES

NOTES

NOTES

_____

_____

_____

_____

_____

_____

_____

_____

_____

_____

_____

_____

_____

_____

_____

_____

_____

_____

CHAPTER NINE

The Weapon of Praise and Worship

Praise is my weapon of choice as a believer. If I know nothing else, I know about praise and worship. This weapon has freed my soul countless times! In times of joy and celebration or in distress I choose to worship and give God praise and focus on what He has done for me. I read the Psalms and encourage my heart! David is one off my favorite people in the Bible because of his brutal honesty with God. He was in different situations and he cried out to God letting Him know how he was feeling. One particular Psalm really ministered to me when I was feeling a little frustrated in my spirit. David was talking to himself wondering why he was upset or feeling cast down. He told himself to wait for God's help. David was a

true worshipper who did not fail to give Jehovah praise for all that He brought him through.
Even though David was not perfect and had his
share of mistakes, he was still a man after
God's own heart. He reminds me of us; we
have fallen down and have made many mistakes but God is patient and cares for us. He
calls us back to Himself.

SOAKING

The definition of this word soaking is -
extremely wet; wet through; to enter or pass
through something by or as if by pores or inter-
stices; to penetrate or affect the mind or feelings. When we "soak" in the presence of the
Lord, we spend uninterrupted time just allowing
God to minister to us. Turning on some worship music that ministers to your spirit is powerful. Artists such as Darrell Evans, Jason Up-
ton, Winston Davenport and Melody Royal
produce soaking music that you can use as
you meditate. During this time of soaking you
are not praying or talking. You are literally

putting yourself in a space for the Holy Spirit to "enter through you and penetrate your mind and feelings." You want to let that time be consumed with being in a relaxed state. You begin by going to a quiet space and lay either on a couch or on the floor with a pillow, be comfortable. It is important that you have no distractions, no phone, computer, television, just you and your music. The reason for soaking is to immerse your soul in whatever Holy Spirit wants to speak to you.

Andre and Kimberly Lefebvre define soaking as,

> 'Taking time to simply be quiet for a few minutes in a day could demand planning and discipline. But what if we would simply "show up" and be silent before God, letting Him pour over us His affection, letting Him reveal our own hearts to ourselves, and as we do, finally learn to become familiar with God's language? In turn, we could just re-

spond by whispering, "Father, I am here to be with you, I let go, I give you, I will do, work in me, heal, save, restore…"'

Our choice to spend time in worship reveals the true person we are. Those flaws that we had been stroking, the weights and the sin that easily besets us, the pet sins we have been nursing all come to the surface. In God's holy presence, sin cannot abide. Those things are exposed giving us the opportunity to release them to God. That is when we willingly let go and allow our Divine Manufacturer go to work to heal our hearts and cleanse us from unright-eousness. He wants to make an exchange; beauty for ashes, the oil of joy for mourning, the garment of praise for the spirit of heavi-ness. He wants to take those things that keep us from having victory and replace them with His strength, peace, joy or whatever it is that we need to obtain freedom from our struggles.

USING OUR HEAVENLY LANGUAGE

When we have been born again we not only receive salvation and eternal life, God has said that if we ask He would give us the gift of the Holy Spirit with the evidence of speaking in other tongues. Let me be clear, though, when we receive Christ as our Savior , the Holy Spirit dwells within us. The late Kenneth Hagin said that the believer who is filled with the Holy Ghost, his tongues are given to him to use constantly in his worship and devotion to God. The Bible says in Acts 10:46 concerning Cornelius and his household when they began to speak with tongues, "For they heard them speak with tongues, and magnify God..." Speaking with tongues is a supernatural way to magnify God.

What songs will you be listening to as you enter in your time of worship? Write down some new artists that you find that minister life to your spirit.

NOTES

_____

_____

_____

_____

_____

_____

_____

_____

_____

_____

_____

_____

_____

_____

_____

_____

_____

_____

_____

_____

_____

_____

NOTES

NOTES

NOTES

FREEDOM FROM FEAR

THE LORD IS THE STRENGTH OF MY LIFE
OF WHOM SHALL I BE AFRAID!
LO, I AM WITH YOU ALWAYS SAY THE
LORD!
GOD DID NOT GIVE ME A SPIRIT OF FEAR!
GOD ORDERS MY STEP, I WILL NOT FEAR!
I AM FULLY EQUIPPED FOR MY ASSIGN-
MENT!
I WILL NOT BE AFRAID OF THEIR FACES!
MY HOPE AND TRUST IS IN CHRIST ALONE!
GOD IS MY SOURCE OF MY LIFE; HE
LEADS ME IN THE DARK PLACES!
I HAVE NO ONE TO FEAR FOR THE
GREATER ONE LIVES IN ME!
I GROW IN GRACE AS I DO GOD'S WILL!
BECAUSE GOD IS LEADING ME I CANNOT
FAIL!

FREEDOM FROM FEAR

I AM DAILY BEING BUILT BY GOD'S WORD!
WHEN DOUBTS FILLED MY MIND, YOUR
COMFORT GAVE ME RENEWED HOPE AND
CHEER. (PSALM 94:19 NLT)
MY CONFIDENCE IS IN GOD!
I AM ALWAYS PROTECTED BY THE ONE
WHO MADE ME!

TOTAL ACCEPTANCE

I AM ACCEPTED IN THE KINGDOM!
I AM COVERED BY THE BLOOD OF THE LAMB!
I AM LOVED BY MY FATHER!
I WILL NOT LIVE BY SIGHT, I LIVE BY FAITH!
GOD IS FAITHFUL!
HE IS THE GIVER OF EVERY GOOD AND PERFECT GIFT!
I AM AN OVERCOMER!
NO WEAPON FORMED AGAINST ME SHALL PROSPER!
I AM NOT ALONE!
GOD'S GRACE IS SUFFICIENT FOR ME!
I SHALL COMPLETE MY ASSIGNMENT NO MATTER WHAT I AM GOING THROUGH!
I WALK IN FAITH AND VICTORY!
MY LIFE IS HIDDEN IN CHRIST!
NO ONE CAN HINDER WHAT GOD HAS SPOKEN FOR MY LIFE!

AFFIRMATIONS

MY FAILURES YESTERDAY ARE LEADING
ME TO MY SUCCESSES, BECAUSE I WILL
NOT QUIT!
I WILL SURROUND MYSELF WITH POSITIV-
ITY!
I WILL NOT BE THE SMARTEST ONE IN THE
ROOM!
I WILL SURROUND MYSELF WITH MOTI-
VATED PEOPLE!
MY SPHERE OF INFLUENCE IS GROWING!
I WILL SPEND TIME READING GREAT
BOOKS!
TELEVISION DOES NOT RULE ME!
I AM LED BY THE SPIRIT OF GOD!
HE ALONE IS MY STRENGTH!
GOD IS THE SUN AND SHIELD WHO GIVES
GRACE AND GLORY; NO GOOD THING WILL
HE WITH HOLD FROM THOSE WHO WALK
UPRIGHTLY!

<u>AFFIRMATIONS</u>

I AM NOT ALONE; THERE ARE MORE WITH
ME THAN THERE ARE THOSE AGAINST ME!
I SPEND TIME BECOMING A BETTER ME;
I AM WORTH THE INVESTMENT!
I AM COVERED BY MY FATHER!
GOD LOVES ME WITH AN EVERLASTING
LOVE!
I AM NOT DEFEATED; I AM MORE THAN A
CONQUERER!
I AM A WINNER!

About the Author

Pastor Darlene Thorne has been devoted to ministry since she was in her early twenties with a desire to impart the word of God to those seeking a life change. This however, has not come without a price. She was raised in a Christian home with her two older sisters and younger brother. Her father was a pastor and her mother was an evangelist. They came together after graduating from Bible college.

After many years of marriage her parents divorced and Darlene was left with a question, "If her parents were believers and their marriage did not last, was God really real and what hope of living a solid Christian life did she really have?" Although she still knew God existed, Pastor Darlene struggled to know of His reality in her life. For some time after her parent's separation, Darlene led a very promiscuous life, she was at odds with her mother and felt abandoned by her father.

Not until she attended a conference which focused on teaching both children and adults how to have a successful and God-filled life, did Pastor Darlene make a total commitment to God and turned her life toward Him. She experienced a new life in Christ that stripped away the bondage and she was delivered from rejection, low-self-esteem and she began to live life with purpose. Her assignment is to encourage women through God's word to live their lives with purpose and not to allow their past to be a hindrance.

As an international speaker, Pastor Darlene has traveled extensively ministering the word of God, speaking at conferences, seminars, workshops and women's meetings. She has a heart for women to be healed and truly be purposeful in their daily lives. To that end, she has authored two books, "A Heart After the Father," a daily devotional and "When Dark Chocolate is Bittersweet". She is presently working on a program entitled, "Slaying the Go-

liath's in Your Life," a series that examines ma-
jor areas in our lives that war against us in our
quest to fulfill our calling and a battle plan to
win against one of our worst enemies, ourselves.

Pastor Darlene has been married to the
love of her life for over 30 years. She and her
husband, Kevin Thorne, serve together as pas-
tors at Grace Worship Center in Clayton, NC.
They have two world changer young adults,
Kevin, II and Kennedy Elayne.

CONFERENCE TOPICS

Some of Pastor Darlene's conference topics are:

* You Weren't Designed to Fit In
* The Me Nobody Knows
* Hiding No More
 * Living Authentically: Embracing the Real You
* How to Personally Invest in Your Dreams

To book Pastor Darlene for your next women's event, conference, workshop or seminar, visit her website:

www.darlenethorne.com

You may also follow her on Instagram, Twitter and Periscope:
@ladydarlenelt

Made in the USA
Middletown, DE
02 February 2023

23700182R00076